# Octopuses and Squids

Text by Mary Jo Rhodes and David Hall
Photographs by David Hall

Undersea Encounters

**Children's Press®**
A Division of Scholastic Inc.
New York   Toronto   London   Auckland   Sydney
Mexico City   New Delhi   Hong Kong
Danbury, Connecticut

Library of Congress Cataloging-in-Publication Data

Rhodes, Mary Jo, 1957-
   Octopuses and squids / Mary Jo Rhodes and David Hall; photographs by David
Hall.— 1st ed.
       p. cm.
   Includes bibliographical references and index.
   ISBN 0-516-24394-2 (lib. bdg.)            0-516-25350-6 (pbk.)
   1. Octopuses—Juvenile literature. 2. Squids—Juvenile literature. I. Hall, David, 1943
Oct. 2- II. Title. III. Series
   QL430.3.O2R49 2005
   594'.56—dc22

                         2005000353

*To the memory of my father, Philip H. Rhodes, for his encouragement, humor, and for
the many beautiful sailboats he designed.*
*—M.J.R.*

*To my wife and diving partner Gayle Jamison, whose sharp eyes have spotted many
a hidden octopus.*
*—D.H.*

All photographs © 2005 David Hall except: Corbis Images/Reuters: 19 inset; Gayle
Jamison: 17 left, 36; Gowlett-Holmes: 3 bottom, 37 bottom; Kim Reisenbichler: 42, 43;
Mark Norman: 32 bottom; Mark Strickland: 18, 19; Mary Malloy: 33 bottom; Minden
Pictures: 8, 32 top, 37 top, 39; Nature Picture Library Ltd./Jeff Rotman: 28; P. Humann:
38 background; Photo Researchers, NY/Alexis Rosenfeld/SPL: 40, 41; Seapics.com/Marilyn
& Maris Kazmers: 33 top.

The chambered nautilus is like a living fossil.
pg. 12

Octopuses are good at making a quick getaway!
pg. 24

# Octopuses and Squids

This female octopus has an unusual way of laying eggs.
pg. 37

Squids have a bullet-shaped body that is designed for speed. They are among the fastest-swimming animals in the ocean.

# chapter 1

# Octopuses, Squids, and Their Relatives

Far below the surface of the ocean lives a mysterious sea animal. No scientist has ever seen or photographed one alive. When it is completely stretched out, this animal is almost as long as a school bus. It is the giant squid.

Squids and octopuses are part of an amazing group of animals called **cephalopods** (SEF-a-low-pods). Cephalopods are **mollusks** (MOL-lusks), distantly related to snails and clams.

They have a head with a mouth surrounded by a circle of arms. Their tongue, called a radula, is covered with tiny teeth.

The bodies of cephalopods are covered with an extra fold of skin called a mantle. It is like a bag that contains the animal's organs. Sticking out from beneath the mantle is the siphon. The siphon looks like a short hose. Through it, water flows in and out of the animal's body.

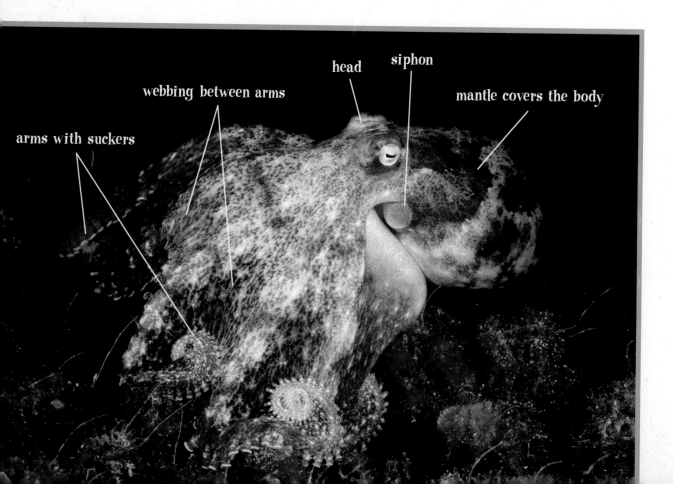

arms with suckers

webbing between arms

head

siphon

mantle covers the body

An octopus has eight arms surrounding its mouth. There is a thin fold of skin, or webbing, between the arms.

# A Shy Giant

The giant Pacific octopus is the world's largest octopus species. It can measure more than 20 feet (6 meters) from one arm tip to another. It is big enough to hug several people at the same time! Although it may look scary, this octopus is shy. It would much rather hide than attack people.

This tiny pygmy squid has attached itself to a blade of seagrass.

Actual Size

## Squids

Squids have smooth bodies that are shaped like a torpedo. They have eight arms plus a pair of long tentacles. Their arms are lined with disks called suckers. Squids are among the fastest-swimming animals in the ocean.

Pygmy squids are the smallest members of the family. A fully-grown adult is about the size of a honeybee. They hide from predators by attaching to the underside of a blade of seagrass.

The largest family member is the giant squid. It can be up to 60 feet (18 m) long. This makes it the largest **invertebrate** (in-VUR-tuh-brate) animal on Earth!

## Octopuses

An octopus does not have a fixed body shape like a squid. Instead, its shape changes constantly. Unlike a squid, an octopus spends most of its life on the ocean floor.

An octopus has eight arms but no tentacles like a squid. The arms surround the octopus's mouth. Inside its mouth the octopus has a hard beak, like a parrot's.

## Octopus Fact

Octopuses and their relatives live in all oceans of the world. Many species (SPEE-seez) can be found in shallow water near the shore. Others, like the giant squid, are found only in the deep ocean.

An octopus can change the shape of its body.

# Chambered Nautilus

Millions of years ago, early cephalopods called ammonites had a heavy outer shell. Today only one family member has such a shell: the nautilus (NAW-til-us).

A nautilus shell has many separate rooms, or chambers. These chambers hold enough air to keep the nautilus from sinking to the bottom of the ocean. The animal itself lives in the largest chamber near the outside. Nautiluses have nearly one hundred tentacles. The nautilus has changed very little in hundreds of millions of years. It is like a "living fossil."

The **fossil** (FOSS-uhl) remains of ammonites can be found in rocks that are hundreds of millions of years old.

This is what a cuttlefish would look like if you came face to face with one.

## Cuttlefishes

The cuttlefish is another cephalopod. It looks like a chubby squid with short arms. Its fins go around its body like a skirt. The cuttlefish has a large, chalky shell inside its body. This shell contains air. It helps the animal to float above the ocean floor. Unlike squids, a cuttlefish usually lives alone and stays near the sea bottom.

Each one of an octopus's eight arms has a double row of white suction disks called suckers.

# chapter 2

# The Intelligent Octopus

An octopus doesn't have a nose to smell with or ears to hear with. It also doesn't have any fingers. So how does this intelligent animal sense the ocean world around it? One way is with its suckers.

## Arms and Suckers

Each octopus arm is lined with a double row of suckers. An octopus may have hundreds of suckers. It can move each one by itself, the way you can move your fingers and toes.

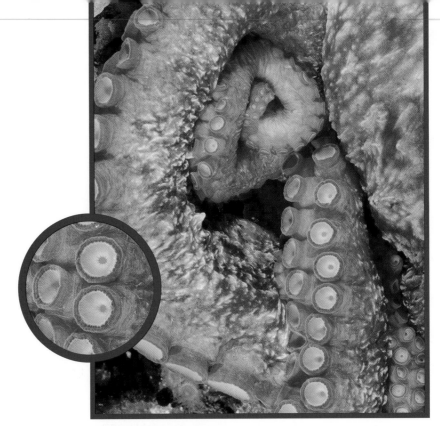

An octopus uses its suckers
to locate prey at night by smell,
taste, and touch.

These suckers act like small suction cups. They can grip objects, as well as feel them. An octopus can even use its suckers for "tasting" the things that it touches.

## Seeing Underwater

Octopuses, squids, and cuttlefishes have very good eyesight. On the outside, their eyes look different from a human's eyes. But on the inside, their eyes are similar to ours.

Octopuses, squids, and cuttlefishes see detailed pictures just as we do. (Other mollusks, such as scallops and some snails, can sense only light and shadow.) They often have large eyes so they can see in dim light. For example, the giant squid has the largest eyes of any animal on Earth. Its eyes are about the size of your head!

Although the eyes of an octopus (left) and a cuttlefish (right) look different from our eyes, they are very similar in structure to our own.

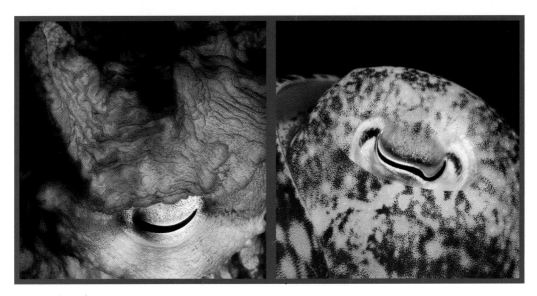

# Smart Cephalopods

Octopuses and cuttlefishes are the most intelligent invertebrate animals. Many experiments have been done to test this idea. Some scientists believe that cuttlefish may be even more intelligent than octopuses. They communicate with one another by using hundreds of different color patterns, such as zebra patterns. These patterns are a kind of "body language."

# The Clever Octopus

Octopuses are able to find their way through mazes. They can even recognize different shapes. In one experiment, an octopus is given a glass jar with a tasty crab inside. Through trial and error, the octopus learns how to unscrew the lid to get at the crab.

By using color patterns on its skin, the male cuttlefish in the middle is warning the male on the right to keep away from its mate.

The octopus is expert at changing shape and color to become almost invisible.

# chapter 3

# Becoming Invisible

Gliding along the ocean floor, an octopus seems to flow like water. It moves easily around rocks and through small openings. An octopus can make its body long and thin like a rope. It can also stretch wide open like an umbrella. It can squeeze itself into amazingly narrow places.

This ability to change shape helps an octopus to sneak up on its **prey** (PRAY). It also helps the octopus to escape from enemies. Because an octopus doesn't have a hard outer shell, it is a tempting meal for a hungry **predator** (PRED-uh-tur).

## Blending In

Octopuses and their relatives are skilled at disguise, or **camouflage** (KAM-uh-flaj). They can change their skin color instantly. Their skin contains small sacs of different-colored **pigments** (PIG-ments). These sacs look like small, colored dots. The dots become larger to darken skin color. They shrink to give the animal a very pale color.

A reef squid is able to make itself appear lighter or darker by changing the size of the colored spots on its skin.

# The Colorful Cuttlefish

One species of cuttlefish does not swim. Instead, it crawls along the bottom with its fins. When it is hunting, it uses camouflage to sneak up on its prey. But when it is threatened, this cuttlefish displays very bright colors. This may serve to warn predators that the cuttlefish is bad-tasting or poisonous.

When it is threatened, the flamboyant cuttlefish becomes brightly colored.

When it is hunting for fish, the same cuttlefish takes on a dull brown color.

By shooting a stream of water out through its siphon, an octopus can quickly "jet" away from danger.

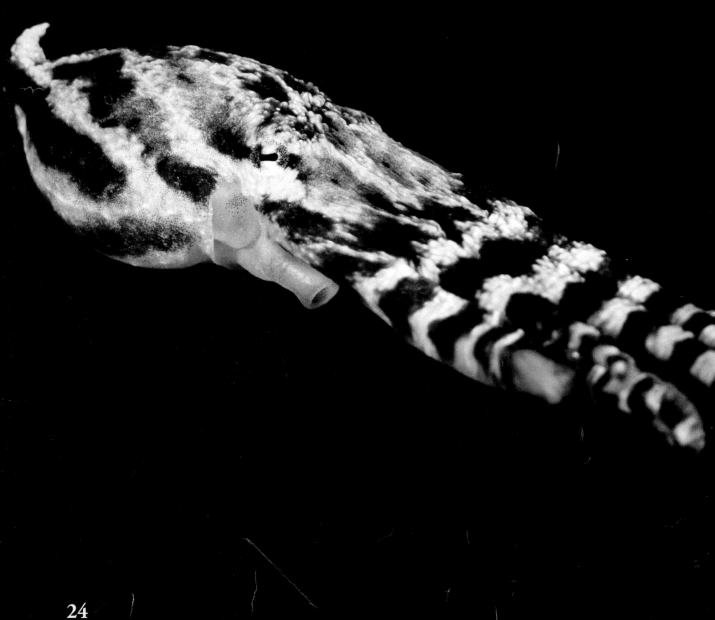

# chapter 4

# Escape Tricks

Octopuses are clever at camouflage. But some predators can still locate an octopus by smell or touch. When this happens, the octopus needs to make a quick escape.

## Jet Propulsion

Octopuses use jet propulsion to escape from danger. If you blow up a balloon and then let it go, the air you put in comes back out. While the air escapes

This cuttlefish is pointing its siphon forward and down. It is ready to jet away if it feels threatened.

rapidly in one direction, the balloon shoots away in the opposite direction.

Octopuses and their relatives use a similar kind of jet propulsion. They suck water into a hollow space around the outside of their body. When they push hard, water is forced out through the siphon. By aiming its siphon carefully, an octopus, squid, or cuttlefish can quickly escape in any direction.

# A Safe Home

To protect themselves from predators during the day, most octopuses have a home called a den. A crack or cave in a rock wall may become a den for a large octopus. A small octopus can hide in an empty clam shell or coconut shell. A really tiny octopus might even live inside an old soda bottle!

Startled by a diver, this giant Pacific octopus releases a cloud of dark ink as it jets away to safety.

## A Smokescreen

If swimming away doesn't work, an octopus or squid has one last trick. It can release black "ink" from its mantle. The ink is a mixture of dark pigment and mucus. It acts like a smokescreen. It can confuse a predator just long enough for the octopus to escape.

### Octopus Fact

Many scientists believe that the mimic octopus twists its arms into different shapes to look like a sea snake, flounder, or lionfish. This behavior helps it to trick predators. It is the only animal that can copy more than one other kind of animal.

# Tiny but Deadly

The blue-ringed octopus is just a few inches long, but it is especially deadly. Its poisonous bite disables crabs and other prey. When it is threatened, it will bite to defend itself. A person bitten by this tiny animal may become very sick or even die.

The blue-ringed octopus is usually camouflaged. But when alarmed, it flashes a pattern of bright, blue rings. This is a warning to others: Keep away!

A Caribbean reef octopus catches a crab by trapping it in the webbing between its outstretched arms.

# chapter 5

# Octopus and Squid Hunters

Most sharks and other large predators hunt during the day. But the cautious octopus waits until after dark before leaving its den to search for food. Octopuses can hunt at night by touch and by smell.

## Searching for Food

Octopuses eat bottom-dwellers, such as crabs, lobsters, and sea snails. They poke the tips of their arms into small

This octopus is holding two crabs in its beak.

openings to search for food. When it locates prey, an octopus stretches open the webbing between its arms like an umbrella. It then pounces and traps the prey beneath its body.

An octopus uses its strong beak and sharp radula as weapons. The radula can be used like a saw to cut off the legs of a crab. It can also be used like a drill to make a hole in the shell of a snail. The octopus injects poison through this hole to kill its prey.

Octopuses often carry prey back to their dens to eat. When an octopus has finished its meal, it places the leftover shells just outside its den. A pile of empty shells may be a clue that an octopus's home is nearby.

This is what the radula of one octopus looks like under a microscope.

## Squid Hunters

Squids do not always sneak up on their prey like octopuses do. Sometimes they chase after them. A squid can swim fast enough to catch most fish.

A squid captures a fish by shooting out its two long tentacles. These are designed for grabbing and holding prey. The squid then uses its sharp beak to kill the fish.

After eating, an octopus often leaves the shell of its prey just outside its den.

Squids are the fastest swimmers of all invertebrate animals. This one has caught a fish.

## Octopus Fact
If a predator bites off an octopus's arm, the octopus can often grow back the missing part.

The female blue-ringed
octopus does not live in
a den. Instead, she carries
her eggs around in the
webbing between her arms.

# chapter 6

# Mothers and Babies

Octopuses prefer to live alone. The only time one octopus interacts with another is when they **mate**. An octopus mates only once in its lifetime.

## Octopus Mating

Before a female octopus lays her eggs, she must first receive **sperm** (SPURM) from a male. Most octopus matings occur during a chance meeting between a male and female. The male octopus has a special

A male reef octopus uses a special arm to deliver his sperm to the female.

arm used for mating. The tip is shaped like a spoon. He uses this long arm to place sperm into the egg duct opening of the female.

The female octopus can store the sperm for several months. When she finally lays her eggs, the male's sperm will **fertilize** (FUR-tuh-lize) them.

## Tending the Eggs

A female octopus may attach her eggs to the roof of her den. She must guard the eggs day and night until they hatch. Usually this takes between four and six weeks. During this time she does not leave her den, not even to hunt for food.

The female uses her siphon to gently squirt water over the eggs. This provides the eggs with the extra oxygen they need to grow. She uses her suckers to keep the eggs clean and healthy.

The female argonaut is the only octopus that makes a shell. She lays her eggs inside the shell, where they will stay until they hatch.

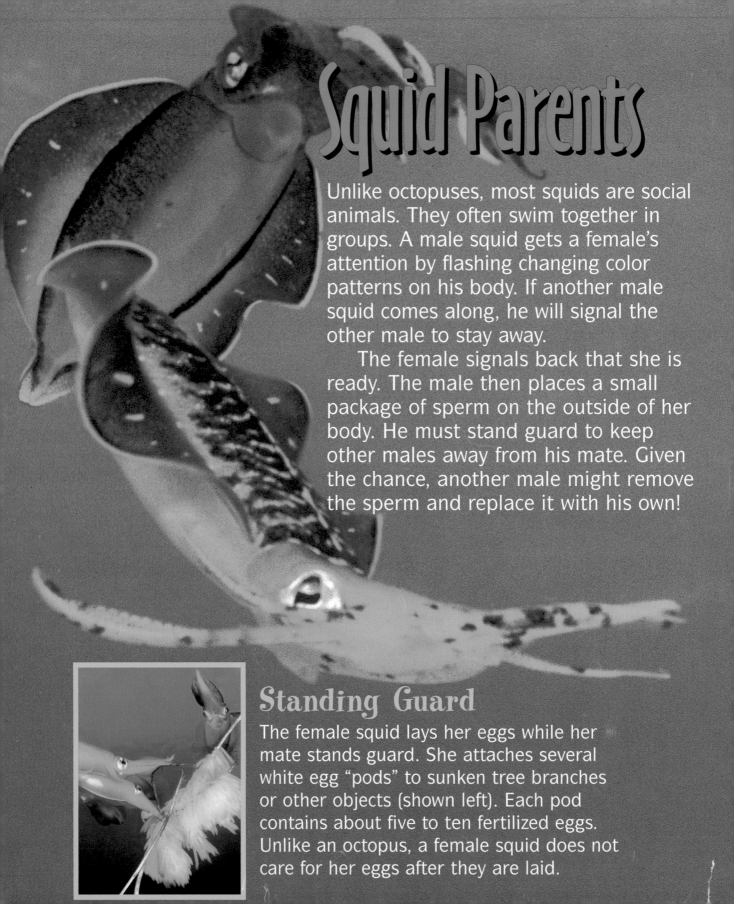

# Squid Parents

Unlike octopuses, most squids are social animals. They often swim together in groups. A male squid gets a female's attention by flashing changing color patterns on his body. If another male squid comes along, he will signal the other male to stay away.

The female signals back that she is ready. The male then places a small package of sperm on the outside of her body. He must stand guard to keep other males away from his mate. Given the chance, another male might remove the sperm and replace it with his own!

## Standing Guard

The female squid lays her eggs while her mate stands guard. She attaches several white egg "pods" to sunken tree branches or other objects (shown left). Each pod contains about five to ten fertilized eggs. Unlike an octopus, a female squid does not care for her eggs after they are laid.

These octopus eggs have begun to hatch. The baby octopuses must quickly learn to take care of themselves.

## Octopus Babies

Soon after her eggs hatch, the mother octopus dies. The baby octopuses are now on their own. They must protect themselves and begin to hunt for food.

Some octopus babies live on the sea floor. Others drift in the ocean for a while. Many of the babies are eaten by other animals. Those that survive settle down on the bottom and grow quickly into adults.

### Octopus Fact

Most octopuses, squids, and cuttlefishes live no longer than one or two years. Some of the smallest ones live just a few months.

This two-person submarine
is used by scientists to
study animals that live in
the deep sea.

# chapter 7

# Deep-Sea Vampires

If you were to travel in a deep-sea vessel, you could go to one of the least explored places on Earth. These small vessels are called **submersibles** (sub-MUR-suh-bulls). They can travel thousands of feet below the surface, where ordinary submarines can't go.

Some unusual cephalopods live in this dark, cold part of the ocean. One of them is called the vampire squid.

The vampire squid lives in water thousands of feet deep, where there is very little light.

## A Vampire's Escape

A vampire squid swims slowly by flapping a pair of fins like wings. It has eight arms and two long, thread-like limbs. These limbs help the vampire squid to sense movement from animals that it can't see in the dark.

Vampire squids are named for the dark webbing between their arms. It looks like a vampire's cape. The webbing also has soft spikes that look like fangs. When threatened, a vampire squid can pull its arms back over its body and hide under the webbing. It seems to turn itself "inside out." In this way the vampire squid can disappear into the darkness.

## Glow-in-the-Dark Vampire

Like a firefly, the vampire squid can create its own light. It produces light through chemical changes within its body. The vampire squid has light organs all over its body that can flash on or off, or glow for several minutes. It does not have an ink sac like other cephalopods that live closer to the surface. But it can eject glow-in-the-dark mucus when it is frightened.

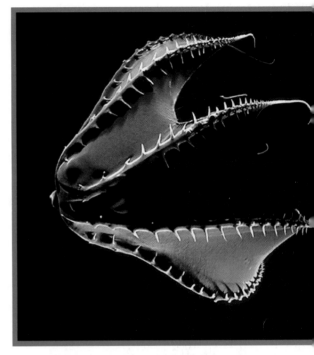

When it senses danger, the vampire squid can fold its arms back over itself and hide beneath its "cape."

Scientists believe that vampire squids use their flashing underwater lights to confuse predators. Many types of squids and other deep-sea animals also create their own light. They use the light for finding food, finding mates, and protecting themselves from predators.

# Glossary

**camouflage** (**KAM-uh-flaj**) the ability of an animal to blend in with its surroundings. *(pg. 22)*

**cephalopods** (**SEF-a-low-pods**) mollusks with many arms surrounding a central mouth. Octopuses, squids, and cuttlefishes are cephalopods. *(pg. 5)*

**fertilize** (**FUR-tuh-lize**) an egg must be fertilized by sperm in order to develop into a baby. This joining of an egg and a sperm is called fertilization. *(pg. 36)*

**fossil** (**FOSS-uhl**) the remains of a plant or animal from long ago, usually preserved in rock. *(pg. 12)*

**invertebrate** (**in-VUR-tuh-brate**) an animal without a backbone. Crabs, starfish, worms, and octopuses are all invertebrates. *(pg. 10)*

**mate** when animals come together to produce offspring. *(pg. 35)*

**mollusks** (**MOL-lusks**) invertebrates with soft bodies, sometimes protected by a hard outer shell. Snails, clams, octopuses, and squids are mollusks. *(pg. 5)*

**pigment** (**PIG-ment**) a natural substance in a plant or animal that gives it color. *(pg. 22)*

**predator** (**PRED-uh-tur**) an animal that hunts and kills other animals for food. *(pg. 22)*

**prey** (**PRAY**) an animal that is killed and eaten by another animal. *(pg. 21)*

**species** (**SPEE-seez**) a particular kind of animal or plant. *(pg. 10)*

**sperm** (**SPURM**) the cells produced by a male animal that can fertilize the eggs produced by a female. *(pg. 35)*

**submersible** (**sub-MUR-suh-bull**) an underwater vessel for exploring the deepest parts of the ocean. *(pg. 41)*

# Learn More About Octopuses and Squids

## Books

Cerullo, Mary. Photographs by Jeffrey Rotman. *The Octopus: Phantom of the Sea.* New York: Cobblehill Books, 1997.

Hunt, James C. *Octopus and Squid.* Monterey Bay Aquarium, 1996.

Norman, Mark. *Cephalopods: A World Guide.* Conchbooks, 2000.

## Magazines

Bavendam, Fred. "Eye to Eye with the Giant Octopus," *National Geographic,* March 1991.

Hanlon, Roger. Photographs by Brian Skerry. "Squid," *National Geographic*, August 2004.

## Web sites

*The Cephalopod Page*
(www.dal.ca/~ceph/TCP/)

*In Search of Giant Squid*
(www.mnh.si.edu/natural_partners/squid4)

*Nature: Incredible Suckers*
(www.pbs.org/wnet/nature/suckers/index.html)

# Index

Note: Page numbers in *italics* indicate illustrations

# About the Authors

After earning degrees in zoology and medicine, **David Hall** has worked for the past twenty-five years as both a wildlife photojournalist and a physician. David's articles and photographs have appeared in hundreds of calendars, books, and magazines, including *National Geographic, Smithsonian, Natural History,* and *Ranger Rick*. His underwater images have won many major awards including *Nature's Best*, BBC Wildlife Photographer of the Year, and Festival Mondial de l'Image Sous-Marine.

**Mary Jo Rhodes** received her M.S. in Library Service from Columbia University and was a librarian for the Brooklyn Public Library. She later worked for ten years in children's book publishing in New York City. Mary Jo lives with her husband, John Rounds, and two teenage sons, Jeremy and Tim, in Hoboken, New Jersey.

# About the Consultant

**Mark Norman** is one of the world's leading experts on cephalopods. He began studying octopuses while working on his Ph.D. and has since discovered more than one hundred new species. Dr. Norman works at the University of Melbourne and the Victoria Museum in Australia. He is author of many scientific papers and of the book *Cephalopods: A World Guide*.